OUTBACK AUSTRALIA

PHOTOGRAPHS FROM THE AUSTRALIAN GEOGRAPHIC IMAGE COLLECTION

CONTENTS

OPPOSITE: *Akubra hat.* MIKE LANGFORD

The trusty Akubra hat has been an icon in Australia for a century, loved by stock hands, farmers and other lovers of the outback's wide open spaces.

One Tree Hotel, Hay Plain, NSW. OLIVER STREWE

Located between Hay and Booligal, this now-restored hotel was built in 1862 as a staging post for Cobb & Co coaches making the journey between the two towns.

INTRODUCTION

The outback. It's hard to define, but you'll know you're there when you've cleared the urban sprawl, relinquished the rural backblocks, and only red dirt and an endless blue sky lie stretched out ahead.

THERE'S NO signpost or map reference. Nor any border to cross. Even though it covers several million square kilometres, what matters here is not a tidy list of locations. In the end, the genius of the outback is that you can't pin it down. To get there you have to head inland and keep travelling. You'll know when it happens.

Every mainland state has a big backyard outside the reach of the usual towns and farms and sealed roads. These are more spaces than places. The terrain is open, flat and arid. Underfoot, the earth is a fiery red and the sky above seems enormous and preternaturally blue. Come midday, the horizon's straggly trees look to be melting ghost-like into the hot, wavering air.

We encounter the outback from many angles. Yet, typically signs of people are scarce and the scenery is slow to change. Being mostly unfenced, the landscapes can appear deserted, even anonymous. In some areas you might travel for half a day — on dusty tracks that often run gun-barrel straight — and not see another car. All of which magnifies an already uncanny feeling of distance and remoteness.

This hypnotic isolation always takes some getting used to. The country's age-worn look and grainy textures challenge our sense of time, our very powers of imagining. However, for all its hardness, the outback is only desolate if you're stuck on what's not there. Wait long enough and there's life in abundance. And when it puts on a show — be it a rumbling summer storm or local race meeting — there's no other world like it.

Moreover, once you get into the swing of the journey, the spaces are strangely addictive. The secret is knowing when to move. In the end the outback is never just about one spot. It's more to do with what's next, and finding ways to relish being out there — out back of beyond.

WILD

Despite our best efforts to tame it, the outback remains nature's stronghold; a place of extremes where life itself can turn on a whim of the weather.

SPRAWLING SALTBUSH and spinifex, floodplains braided with powder-dry channels, expanses of brigalow scrub and mulga woodland, salt pans, dunefields and gibber flats in boundless arrays. Here, landscape is a rolling sea of patterns and abstract surfaces — a rhythm wonderfully evoked in the Aboriginal art of the western deserts.

Across this vastness the climate is anything but routine. Dry times can stretch for years. Furious dust storms and thunderheads come out of nowhere. Life turns on the whim of two seasons: boom and bust. To see out lean times demands a knack for invention and for lying low.

This is the empire of reptiles, insects and tiny mammals; creatures who graft a living among cracks and shadows. Dingoes and mobs of emus and red kangaroos follow the wind, roaming wide for the last tufts of grass, scraps and the drying soaks.

But every decade or so there's a freakish summer when the rains never stop. Rafts of heavy monsoon cloud keep coming. Creeks and billabongs splay out across the land. Within days the country is lush and green. A thrum of bird calls and frog notes fills the air. Another reminder there's no space on Earth wilder than the outback.

OPPOSITE: *Frill-necked lizard.* STEVE WILSON
With an exciting display in which it fans out its 20cm-diameter frill, this is one of Australia's most spectacular lizards. It's found in tropical woodlands.

Termite mound and ghost gum, Mataranka, NT. BILL BACHMAN
A red termite mound and ghost gum stand resplendently in a sea of brown spear grass
near Mataranka, 300km south-east of Darwin.

Sturt Creek, Canning Stock Route, WA. JEFFERY DREWITZ
Smooth-barked coolibahs slake their thirst in an ephemeral lake along the northern
section of this legendary stock route.

Brumbies near Lake Gregory, WA.

ANDREW GREGORY

Feral brumbies and their foals run freely by Lake Gregory, which changes from being a dry salt pan to a desert lake teeming with birds.

Western grey kangaroo, Mungo NP, NSW. BARRY SKIPSEY
Its 80cm tail stretched out behind it, a western grey kangaroo pauses atop an ancient sand
dune. Western greys are found from south-western Queensland to southern WA.

Wild camel, NT. BARRY SKIPSEY
An awesome sight in the outback, camels have been part of the landscape since explorers
used them in the mid-19th century. There are now more than a million feral camels.

Plumed whistling-ducks, NT. DAVID HANCOCK

Easily identified by long flank plumes that extend over its back, the plumed whistling-duck
is widespread in the tropical north and eastern states, and makes spirited staccato whistles.

Dingo, Tanami Desert, NT. BILL BACHMAN
Inquisitive and crafty, a dingo keeps eyes and ears peeled among the spinifex
of the Tanami Desert in the NT.

Lesser hairy-footed dunnart, Ethabuka Reserve, Qld. NICK RAINS
Dunnarts are carnivorous native marsupials that look a little like mice. The lesser
hairy-footed dunnart is common in the Simpson Desert.

Honeypot ant, Central Deserts, NT. MITCH REARDON
Its abdomen swelled to the size of a grape, this honeypot ant has been fed with nectar
collected by fellow ants. When food is scarce, other ants will feed on the honey.

Red kangaroos, Sturt NP, NSW. MITCH REARDON
The largest of the kangaroos, big reds can stand 1.4m tall, with a tail length
of another 80cm. Males may reach 90kg in weight.

Lake Pamamaroo, Menindee Lakes, NSW. BILL HATCHER
Dead red gums stand in Lake Pamamaroo, part of the Menindee Lakes Water
Storage System that supplies Broken Hill in far western NSW.

TAMED

The outback's vastness and its oft times hostile nature demands resourcefulness and ingenuity of those who dare to call it home.

WE CAN make tracks and set up camps. It's no problem to run a few sheep or sink bores. With enough push we can create entire towns or the machinery to mine a mountain flat. Of course the outback can be tamed — but only for so long.

All around Australia's desert fringes there are relics: from abandoned homesteads and long-fallen fences to buckled windmills creaking in the breeze. When droughts hit hardest, the ore's no more, or your luck runs out, there's nothing to do but go.

By dint of stubbornness, and sometimes sheer scale, settlements and stations do hang on. Yet, for most, success in the outback is all about the art of journey making. Following seasons and natural cycles has been at the heart of the success of Aboriginal cultures for many thousands of years — and a skill that helped found our cattle industry.

We've learned to survive by spanning monumental distances. With camel trains and droving routes, our overland telegraph and train lines, there have been victories, of sorts. We even managed to cross the continent with a dog fence and learn that the best place to station the local doctor is in a plane. Slowly and stoically we've got the outback's measure. But only a stranger to its vastness would ever dream of holding the upper hand.

OPPOSITE: **Miner, Lightning Ridge, NSW.** GRAHAME MCCONNELL
A miner in western NSW prepares to go searching for precious opals among the sandstone and clay underground at Lightning Ridge.

Delta Downs, Karumba, Qld. MURRAY SPENCE
In the Gulf Country of Queensland, an Aboriginal stockman continues a heritage of several
generations of Aboriginal stockmen, at the indigenous cattle station Delta Downs.

Shearing time, Curnamona station, SA. MIKE LANGFORD
It's 7.30 am and shearing has just begun at Curnamona station. Shearers in Jacky Howes
slide the woolly backs onto the boards and the wool begins to fall.

Old wagon wheel, Lightning Ridge, NSW. GRAHAME MCCONNELL
There's often an elegant beauty and untold stories in the detritus of yesteryear strewn
through the outback, such as this grand old timber-spoked wheel.

Water tank and windmill, Docker River area, NT. PETER MCNEILL
Under a vast outback sky painted splendidly with golds and reds, a windmill slowly pumps
water from under the surface of this dry land near the NT–WA border.

Rice paddies, Riverina District, NSW. MIKE LANGFORD
Looking for ducks feeding on recently sown grain, an ultralight buzzes over rice
paddies at Talinga in southern NSW.

Artesian bore, Simpson Desert, Witjira NP. SA. EDWARD STOKES
Gushing out of the desert at near boiling point, water rises 1400m from the
Great Artesian Basin. The bore was drilled in 1963, but has since been capped.

Miners' lamps, Lightning Ridge, NSW. GRAHAME MCCONNELL
Lights for previous generations of miners, these rusting relics hang on a corrugated iron
structure that has stood the test of time in the opal-mining town of Lightning Ridge.

Opal mining, Lightning Ridge, NSW. GRAHAME MCCONNELL
Second-generation miner Steve Bevan chips away at a sandstone and clay wall in search of
opals on the New Coocoran Opal Fields.

The Ghan, NT.

THOMAS WIELECKI

The Ghan glides 2979km across the Red Centre between Darwin and Adelaide in just 60 hours. It's named after the Afghan cameleers who first plied the route.

Road train, Strzelecki Track, SA. BILL BACHMAN
More than 20 road trains ply this 475km, dusty track daily, a route that links Lyndhurst
with Innamincka through the Strzelecki Desert.

Road train, Tennant Creek, NT. THOMAS WIELECKI
Keno, a blue heeler, stands guard over his master's rig outside the Threeways Roadhouse
along the Stuart Highway, colloquially known as "The Track".

PLACES

With names that evoke misty-eyed nostalgia for pioneering days, outback towns, tracks and cattle stations are the stuff Aussie legends are made of.

THERE ARE the back country towns of legend. Historic hubs like Bourke, Kalgoorlie, Longreach and Port Augusta. Perched on the crossroads to the interior, they're staging posts and busy supply centres for vast swathes of the continent.

Deeper inland there's a roll call of quintessentially outback haunts. Their names alone evoke a vivid and quirky remoteness: Oodnadatta, Tibooburra, Parachilna, Boulia, Innaminka, William Creek and, perhaps most famously of all, Birdsville. Some are little more than wayside stops. Others are roguish one-pub towns where no one blinks if you arrive on a camel or park your plane at the front door.

Yet such outposts are only rarely a final stop. For most visitors their true destination is an overland crossing like the Tanami Track or Canning Stock Route. These ramblings are punctuated by all manner of landmarks, from monumental Uluru to chimeras such as Lasseter's Reef.

With their quests and visions these modern-day pilgrimages carry faint echoes of this land's ancient living pathways — the Dreaming trails through time and space that have sustained Aboriginal Australia for thousands of years. Trails summoned by story and song, and vital with creation and ancestral beings. They point us to the protean essence of the outback as a place to keep discovering; a place of the spirit.

OPPOSITE: **Wedge-tailed eagle, Sturt NP, NSW.** MITCH REARDON
Emblem of the Corner Country, Australia's largest eagle species surveys the Mitchell grass plains between Tibooburra and Wanaaring, close to where NSW, Queensland and SA meet.

Art Gallery, Silverton, NSW. BILL HATCHER
Silverton, a former booming mining town, is today a magnet for visual artists like Peter
Browne whose emu caricatures painted on abandoned VW's have been seen worldwide.

Louisa Downs station, Kimberley, WA. MIKE LANGFORD
Amid swirling dust, penned Kimberley cattle are loaded through the race onto a road train.
The cattle industry remains a vibrant part of vast outback areas.

Birdsville Hotel, Birdsville, Qld. COLIN BEARD
Accident-prone Boss, a kelpie-blue heeler cross, poses in his favourite spot, on the road in
front of the legendary Birdsville Hotel, at the northern end of the Birdsville Track.

Curdimurka, SA. FRANCES MOCNIK
In camps of friends and family, revellers gather for the Curdimurka Outback Ball, an event
held every two years at an abandoned rail siding on the old Ghan line.

Woolshed,
Mt Lyndhurst
Station, SA.

BILL BACHMAN

One of Australia's
largest sheep
stations, 3500sq.km
Mt Lyndhurst was
established in 1869.
In its heyday up
to 54 blade shearers
worked the boards
in the stone
woolshed.

Argyle diamond miner, Kimberley, WA. MIKE LANGFORD
Since 1983, workers at the Argyle Diamond Mine have excavated ancient creek beds where
diamonds, including the valuable pink variety, have been washed down over time.

The Kidman Way, western NSW. PHILLIP GOSTELOW
On the Kidman Way out of Bourke, western NSW, graziers occasionally use the green pick
by the roadside for their stock.

Lightning Ridge, NSW. GRAHAME MCCONNELL
Diving into the spirit of an outback town, the people of Lightning Ridge dug deep to raise
the $300,000 they needed in 1990 to build an Olympic-sized public pool.

The Birdsville Track, SA. COLIN BEARD
Graham Childs, 26, from Cessnock NSW, humps his bluey down the 500km Birdsville Track
near Mungeranie, SA. "I've trained myself to live off the land," he said.

Cravens Peak Reserve, Qld.

NICK RAINS

A former cattle
station, Cravens
Peak became a vast
western Queensland
reserve in 2005.
Some 2236sq.km
in size, it contains
desert dunes,
wetlands, mountain
ranges and open
channel country.

FACES

Masters of making do. Scholars of struggle. The people of the outback wear countenances etched with the experience of this harsh and unyielding land.

OUT HERE every face has tales to tell. There's no masking the effects of the elements. As a result, faces become creased maps — signatures of a life under bright, implacable skies.

Being remote keeps people alone and apart, but that seclusion also creates its own ties. When neighbours do gather, their celebrations and sporting contests are legendary. Isolation works as an unspoken, binding force. If somebody's stranded or in strife, help happens, no questions asked, no worries mate.

The people of the outback have learned to be steady, tight-lipped and frugal with emotion. A dry, knockabout humour is like a forcefield against myriad disappointments. At times this life seems too absurdly serious not to laugh.

In so much unpopulated terrain the very act of seeing another face — a glimpse of a fellow traveller — can be an event in itself. Under hats like dust-streaked outcrops, these faces, with their wizened grins and faraway looks, chart a world hard won.

Whether stubbled and sun flaked, daubed in ochre, or grizzled with grime, the face of the outback is a group portrait of dogged hope and humility shared. Yet more signals that out here only the authentic survive.

OPPOSITE: **Carol Green Napangardi, Tanami Desert, WA.** BILL BACHMAN
Ten-year-old Lajamanu resident Carol Green Napangardi is painted up in the colours of the local Aussie rules team.

Earl Gano, gold miner, Pine Creek, NT. DAVID HANCOCK
On the outskirts of Pine Creek, in the Top End, Earl Gano stands in front of the only
steam-powered stamp battery in the NT, used to crush rock.

Tanami Downs, NT. BILL BACHMAN
Sophie and Callum Parbury play atop a termite mound on
4200sq.km Tanami Downs station.

Hazel Bird, Gemfields, Qld. NICK RAINS
Hazel Bird flashes a smile, her teeth set with diamonds and
sapphires from the Central Queensland Gemfields.

Greg Beaton and sons, Corner Country, NSW. MITCH REARDON

Greg Beaton, one-time supervisor of the 584km NSW section of the 5300km dog fence that runs between SA and NSW, with fellow bushies, sons Jo and Don.

Linda and Jack O'Rafferty, Kimberley, WA. MIKE LANGFORD
In golden light, Linda and her son Jack O'Rafferty (15 months) play with water in a
mango orchard, part of the Ord River irrigation scheme.

Mick McCormick, bull-rider, NSW. GRAHAME MCCONNELL
Bull-rider Mick McCormick takes time out after a kick from
a bucking bronco, or buckjumper, catches him in the face.

Debbie Roberts, Napperby station, NT. BILL BACHMAN
Originally from Cowwarr, Victoria, 22-year-old Debbie
Roberts found work on this 5700 sq. km. cattle station.

Trevor Davis of Tom Groggin station, Upper Murray Valley, NSW. BILL BACHMAN
This historic station was the home of the legendary stockman Jack Riley, who was
arguably the inspiration for AB "Banjo" Paterson's *The Man from Snowy River.*

Beasts of Burden, Brunette Downs Station, NT. DEAN SAFFRON
Heat and flies on the Mitchell and Flinders grass plains prove too much for a young steer as
stockman "Tick" Everett hitches him to the back of his mount for the journey home.

Noel Fullerton, camel consultant, NT. BARRY SKIPSEY
Senior statesman for the Australian camel industry, Noel regularly travels to the Middle
East to advise Arab camel breeders and trainers.

· 57 ·

Anangu youngsters Cecil and Lachlan Brady, SA. BARRY SKIPSEY
The Anangu-Pitjantjatjara Yankunytjatjara lands of northern SA are a treasury of secrets
and songs. The area's relative inaccessibility has helped preserve Anangu culture there.

Tom O'Driscoll, farrier, Beaudesert, Qld. DEAN SAFFRON
Tom performs a job done through the ages, but his tools of
the trade include the best of modern technologies.

Willie Kooma, camel man, Qld. RUSSELL SHAKESPEARE
Willie rounds up feral camels on bush properties around
Outback Queensland, trekking up to 50km in a single day.

Country Women's Association (CWA) members, Qld. FRANCES MOCNIK
Isabelle Kearney, Janelle Cole and Shirley Branch sell homemade wares at the
Ruth Fairfax Building in Brisbane named for the CWA's first president.

Santa Claus, aka Michael Harrison, Tibooburra, NSW. SAGE
In red country a long way from the North Pole, a dinkum Santa joins the bush Christmas
organised for local School of the Air students by Tibooburra's branch of the CWA.

OUTBACK AUSTRALIA

PHOTOGRAPHS FROM THE AUSTRALIAN GEOGRAPHIC IMAGE COLLECTION

All the photographs featured in this book can be ordered as high quality photographic prints.
For details and prices, please visit **www.australiangeographicprints.com.au**

MANAGING EDITOR, AUSTRALIAN GEOGRAPHIC COMMERCIAL: Chrissie Goldrick
BOOK DESIGN: Mike Rossi   CREATIVE DIRECTOR: Andrew Burns
WRITERS: Quentin Chester, Ken Eastwood, Chrissie Goldrick
SUB-EDITOR: Josephine Sargent   PROOFREADER: Nina Paine
PRODUCTION MANAGER: Victoria Jefferys   PREPRESS: Klaus Müller

AUSTRALIAN GEOGRAPHIC GENERAL MANAGER: Jo Runciman
AUSTRALIAN GEOGRAPHIC EDITOR: Ian Connellan

MANAGING DIRECTOR: Matthew Stanton   PUBLISHING DIRECTOR: Gerry Reynolds
PUBLISHER: Andrew Stedwell   CEO, NINE ENTERTAINMENT CO.: David Gyngell

Printed in China by Everbest Printing Co.Ltd.
© ACP Magazines Ltd 2012

Published by ACP Magazines Ltd, 54–58 Park Street, Sydney, NSW 2000
Australian Geographic customer service 1300 555 176 (Australia only)

www.australiangeographic.com.au

AUTHOR: Chester, Quentin.
TITLE: Outback Australia : images from the Australian Geographic image collection / Quentin Chester, Ken Eastwood, Chrissie Goldrick.
ISBN: 9781742453194 (hbk.)
SUBJECTS: Australian Geographic Pty. Ltd.-Pictorial works. Landscape photography-Australia, Central--Pictorial works.
OTHER AUTHORS/CONTRIBUTORS: Eastwood, Ken. Goldrick, Chrissie. Australian Geographic Pty. Ltd.
DEWEY NUMBER: 919.4291

Other titles in the series Photographs from the Australian Geographic Image Collection:
Australia in Colour, Landscapes of Australia, Australia's Coast

---

FRONT COVER:

Docker River, NT

PETER MCNEILL

Under a fiery outback sky stands a lone windmill — one of the enduring symbols of the outback.

TITLE PAGE:

Curdimurka, SA

FRANCES MOCNIK

A dancing duo swing into action at an outback ball under the stars on the old Ghan railway line at Lake Eyre South, SA.

BACK COVER:

Birdsville Track, SA

COLIN BEARD

Legendary bushie "the man in the red hat" was tracked down by an Australian Geographic team on the Birdsville Track, and revealed to be Graham Childs, from Cessnock, NSW.